Poetry in Progress

by

Anna Molly

ISBN: 978-1-957244-18-1

Pirate Farms Books paperback edition / November 2022

Dedication

This book is dedicated firstly to my sister, who wouldn't take "I don't know about this" for an answer, and secondly to my poetry-ambivalent husband who said, "Do it. Someone will like it."

Acknowledgements

I'd like to give a special thanks to Kelly and Holly for feedback and formatting.

Forward

I began thinking about publishing my poetry sometime during the spring of 2020. What else was there to do? I talked with my sister about it, and it went something like this:

> Me: I really like poetry.

> Her: You should publish some of yours.

> Me: (Sigh) But does anyone really read poetry anymore? I mean, I want them to! But do they?

> Her: Publish it anyway.

The idea sat there on the backburner. I really want people to love poetry again, and I thought maybe the more of us who publish it, the more it'll be out in the world to entice people to love it. That thought at least kept the idea on a burner instead of just totally chunked in the dumpster.

Then, for Christmas that year, my sister gave me a shove in the form of pens, flash drives, and a binder with a cover she drew (she's a great artist!) entitled "Poetry in Progress" with the intent that I would get it (read: myself) together, type up my poetry (I have several handwritten journals of the stuff), and then publish it all under some appropriate title. Her title was meant to indicate the work-in-progress phase. But what is creativity of any kind if not always in progress? I think some people are scared of poetry because it seems hard to master—both in writing it and interpreting it. I decided that I wanted to keep her title (and artwork) to show people that, while it does take work, you do progress. Some poems will be better than others; people will differ about which they think are better. And that's okay.

Sometimes you feel like you wrote a great poem only to hate the one you write the next day. That's okay, too. I want people to know that you don't just wake up writing masterpieces.

To that end, I've included poems from my earliest years of serious poetry writing—not the "Buggy wuggy was a bug, but buggy wuggy had no blood, so buggy wuggy wasn't buggy, or wuggy?" kind of thing I started with at age five, but things I started writing when I got serious about it. There are poems here about so many different things—not necessarily what I've experienced but also things I've seen others going through. Poetry is a great medium for expressing feelings of empathy (so, yeah, not every poem is about me or even people I know) as well as feelings about your own experiences. And, yeah, I was a morbid kid—you have been warned—but there's much of light and love and beauty in here, too.

I'm no Shakespeare, Frost, or Gorman, but if you find just one poem you like, then I'll be happy. Better yet, if it inspires just one person to want to write poetry, then I can die happy (seriously, if it inspires you, send me an email; I'd hate to die a sad old lady with unfulfilled dreams, and surely you wouldn't want that on your conscience), for what better way is there to express the kind of pain that makes you scream into the void, the frustration when your society does something stupid and swears they meant to do it, or the marvelous wonder of hummingbirds and dragonflies and nature's evening light show that is fireflies?

Prologue
The High School Years

I've included this as an example of early poetry writing. Be kind, I was an angsty kid.

The Drop
2/20/89

Falling, sailing
     toward the stop
   not waiting
colors flowing
    In and out
   unguided

-- Cascading down a mountain top

I wonder
I watch

Drop splashes down
     rings surround
   moving out
now as one
     with all love
   expounded

-- Flowing through a wooded glade

I die
I live

2

It Rose
2/20/89

White crystal floor
     of clear, cold castle
and unseen door
     -- Out stepped I
then looking in
     on powder floor

     It rose

Base of green
     out life, it poured
Up rising high
     -- unadorned
Top of red
     unfolded

     it Rose

The Crystal Palace
2/21/89

Flowers drowning
      Youth mislaid
I saw the sun
        when I was dead
I looked through glass
      on inside turn
And saw the world
        hoped it would burn
—The day of green so quickly fades
      to be replaced
        by lines of grey—
And falling
      ever-longing
ol time we should not find
      I know upon the morn
        Of the place in which I die

~And the crystal palace rose~

Deer I did see
      Hunter's blood
Fell on its knees
        gave a great shove
Rain poured down
      upon the land
And covered the world
        death grip of hand
—The rain it stopped the death tirade;
      it did not shine
        the night away—
Moon shining
        forever-glow

4

Time that's quickly coming
      The morrow will I mourn
            the flowers which are dying

~And the crystal palace cracked~

Simple minded
      never seen
She saw the sun
        where I had been
The flower rose
      in fullness bloomed
dried and cracked
        For it I yearned
—The night stole in on quiet feet
     to take the light
        and live the day—
Lost my grip
        holding-falling
of time that we have found
     morrow I mourn no more
        the darkness of crying sound

~And the crystal palace crashed~

Butterflies
4/18/89

Butterflies drift down
on cool winds of summer's life
Sit back calm
and watch the world
devoid of care

The Gathering
11/13/89

The sound rings through the walls.
The players pick up guitars.
A hush falls on the crowd
as the first sound comes through loud.

All eyes are turned to the players.
The people pile close in layers.
The crowd picks up the tune,
and they're singing very soon.

The lights in the room hang low,
emitting a warm, soft glow.
The world goes on outside,
and the people 'come alive.

The night approaches dawn;
And the guitars, with their songs, play on.

The Rose
12/89

I opened the door carelessly and flit into the room.
The sun was down and the sky was dark—
      a symbol of my doom.

I threw the stuff down on the bed
and turned to catch the light.
My eye was caught on my dresser top—
      And something was not right.

I noticed what was wrong before the second was all up.
The vase was empty on my dresser—
      the rose had not curled up.

The rose was gone without a trace,
leaving the empty vase.
The leaves were scattered on the counter—
      a petal at the base.

My love is gone forever, dead to the world beyond.
The emptiness has come upon me—
      Forever severed bond.

The Living Dead
1990

Out in the quiet dark of night
a shattering sound echoes
and the deep blue splinters part to black,
fall like shards onto the broken glass
and drip blood from the blades;
rains blood from the blackless pit
and crumbles all apart
as the light of the window dies,
goes black, and fills red;
becomes dead,
knows it's wrong,
and joins the living dead.

Claytonia Virginica
2/22/90

Into the wind went blowing seeds—
seeds of morning time.
Dew drops swell and drop from leaves,
the leaves of morning light.
The flowers of tomorrow open their petals
and look on yesterday,
knowing the grass swayed then
and will continue to sway.
The cotton from the cotton trees,
the pollen from the flowers;
the fragrance from the grass and leaves,
and multi-colored petals;
the lightly blowing breeze
of balmy, warm, soft air,
leaves nothing to my thoughts of winter
and the worse despair.

The Wheel and Loom
3/2/90

The light that came
was from the walls.
The empty rooms
and vacant halls
left the girl confused
and wary.
She could not think
of where she was,
no thought of whence she came.
Endless halls to endless rooms,
and all of it white,
but dark for thought.
She walked from room
to empty room,
and then she saw the wheel and loom.
Not one chair stood in the room,
no table nor a bed;
just the spinning wheel and loom.
The wheel was empty,
but the loom—
it had a thread
woven through
with broken end
dipped in red.

The Faerie Song
3/9/90

I.

A lazy day
in the mid of May
the dew drops fell
at home,

and little wings
of sprites and things
did glisten in
the morn.

A rainbow grew
on a web of dew,
and the sun rose
to noon.

The flittering
of golden wings
sent light around
the wood.

Transparent ones
 went out in the sun
and played their games
till night.

II.

A human form
struck out at morn,
the faerie hill
to find.

He walked all day
to where the hill lay
and watched for sprites
and gnomes.

The faerie songs
reached him ere long,
and he did stake
the hole.

As they approached,
the man bent and crouched—
to spring.

The faeries screamed,
and some took wing;
the rest—they died
of grief.

III.
The sun did set
and out slowly crept
the beings of
the night.

The sprite stepped out
making no sound
to see if all
was right.

In silent nights
glow dim, doused lights
of flitting wings

at play;

the silent games
and mournful dreams
 of faeries left
no days.

The laughing song,
now forever gone
from rainbows, dew,
and light.

Chapter 1
The College Years

Where some improvements are made, but the angst still lives.

Transcendentalism
8/10/90

Waiting for the light to come
and knowing that it won't,
I sit in darkness in my room
knowing that I don't.

Passive Suicide
8/11/90

falling down—
      an endless hole.
drowning in the darkness.
black liquid—
      forcing death of hope.

~and waiting for the sun to come, I see a hint of hope,
then falter, slip, and fall below~

      an endless realm of nothingness,
      a place to sit and wait,
      watching for the saving grace;
      knowing it's too late.

Life In a Dream
8/17/90

When into the night a bubble blows
with rainbows.
Trapped inside and looking out
and floating on the breeze,
no way to leave.
    To change the scene,
    to change the time,
      to change life.
Flowers five feet tall fly by,
and plant in the distant wood.
A blue-it,
gossamer wings blue in the night,
stabs a staff at the bubble shell,
and flits on by.
    But the bubble does not break.
    It cannot break.
    It is fragile
      and hard,
      and holds forever.
Live enclosing life
will not give up its shape.
Bounce along the blades of grass,
sleeping form inside
    and
babbles on forever by the stream
    and
with the stream.
    A tree,

an oak,
a willow by its side.
    Reach out
    to grab
    and hold
    and stop
  but can't.
Not long enough to make a difference.
Daisies float by
and laugh
and giggle
and watch the floating zoo,
its solitary cage.
A faerie comes and peers inside
and tries to help
  but
    dies
over hills and in far aways.
    And ways
    so far
    we'll never find,
    gone long distant.
      Where the bubble goes.
That's where it goes.
      And goes.
And floats along the grassy woods
and watery plains,
along the forested rivers,
lost among the changes it cannot change.

An Idea
9/10/90

Wind blows hard, driving the rain.
Dark turmoil of the sky, rumbling blackness
raging around a grey solid
in a green sea of emerald.
A shadow wavers through the rain,
fading through the torment of the torrent,
struggling to be, and swept away
by the force of its opposition.

Lost Girl
9/28/90

Upon the hill at night I felt
a presence stand beside me.
Looking over, there I saw
a little girl in a blue dress.
She looked at me with doleful eyes,
and reached to take my hand.
I slipped my hand around her hand
and squeezed it very gently.
We sat upon the hill till dawn,
comforting the child who slept in my arms.
I fell asleep just 'fore sunrise,
and woke to morning light.
Looked down into my empty arms
and cried for lack of sight.

Lost for Words
9/28/90

A tinkling sound of words that fall
    and crash upon the ground
        pervades my senses and my thoughts.
The shattered pieces lie around
    the floor and scattered by my feet
        in hopes that I shall pick them up
           and make them whole again.
But my mind, which sees all this,
    has no disturbing desire
        to pick up someone else's pieces
           and put them back together
               when I'd rather make a fire.
I see the melting verbs and nouns,
    all their descriptive words,
      and wonder why they break for me,
        why don't I understand?
           Instead, gather them in piles
              and watch them sadly burn.

Dark Winds
10/19/90

Dark winds blow
across the vacant soul
of a long dead hope.

Dream
11/27/90

Dream
a dream
I dream
I don't.

Fairie Forest
1991

Drop! Splish!
The tinkle of a bell-flower on the shore,
A long, heavy-at-the-bottom-wide-and-thin-at-the-top
seed drop-spinned to the ground
as little eyes sparkled up and a giggle echoed in the
wood.
Flowing fuzz drifts through the air,
and little blues flit here and there.
A red and white-dotted mushroom drips dew over its
side
in the morning glow of a bright sunrise.
Colors prism through the sides
as, hands cupped to catch a drink, a sprite
hums a little tune.
A butterfly all blue and gold sits in the hands of a wood
nymph old.
The rings of water, clear as glass, spread to the banks of
soft, green grass
as the frog who hopped swims to the shore
to try again.

Loves Lost
1/29/91

Take the symbol
from its shelf.
Watch it fall
      and break the shell.
No damage done
that can't be fixed—
only the love
      that leaks from the well.

Depressing Sonnet Number One
9/3/91

Alone, he walks along a silent road.
A whisper straining toward hollow ears
will never reach the distance of his mind.
He gives up struggling, shedding empty tears.
A darkness descends upon his bleak world—
daylight to night, snow into ashes; grey.
He desperately fights weeds that are gnarl'd,
while searching, looking around for his way.
Not finding his path, he lies down to die
apart from the world, devoid of all life.
A smile on his lips, and closing his eyes,
he pleasantly ceases to be alive.

On a clear day as the light slowly goes,
they realize his life has come to a close.

Virtual Life Lessons
9/13/91

Try to find the answers
in a small square box.
No window to the real world,
and a door that's always locked.

Train us for the real world
but not through living it.
Show us films and movies,
as if it should make sense.

Screaming in the dark room
as they sit content inside.
Destroy the life projector,
knowing the answers are outside.

The doors unlock.
They spill us into the world.
Blinking in the reality,
lost, and never knowing why.

Forging a Friendship
9/17/91

Forest deep
        and wand'ring wood,
We wandered down the creek;
and every water-bug and fish
delightful to our eyes.
The stars so bright in dark night skies
        clear from cities light.
Found a place to sit awhile
and hear the sounds of life—
crickets, frogs, birds, and tadpoles
and aardvarks as armadillos.
Winds blow the trees
so high above—
our imagination making them demons.
We play awhile in childish fancy,
gaze into the stars
        and see one shooting down.
Time for us to go—
our flashlight grows dim—
so we wander our way
back to camp
with visions of caves
tomorrow.

Toast
10/2/91

Numbness,
my arms first.
They are lightweight, yet not.
It spreads
to my legs, my shoulders and neck are sore,
heavy with the weight of my head.
My head goes.
I am tired.
Agitated.
Frustrated.
Concentration is a game.
Writing is hard, messy, child-scribble.
Don't forget to breathe!
Am I breathing?
My mind is not on lecture, notes.
The thought police will be here soon.
A vague fear of unknown
creeps up in my mind.
What is there?
What's going to happen to me?
Something bad; I'm sure they're out there!
  Waiting
  Waiting
In the ice-palace
the signal
They can see me
They know I am not taking notes.
They know I'm writing a poem about them.
They'll come for me 'cause I'm the only one who knows
who they are.
I fumble with my glasses.
My God! I see the board

There are words there.
The lights are upside down spaceships.
Monsters are real because I thought of them.
Some D-man says so, too.
My arms.
My arms feel restless they want to run
        away
but my legs won't take them
and my shoulders won't let them go anyway.
I scream.
Somewhere in the depths of my mind
my mouth is dry.
I have to get away from this.
I have to get away from it.
It?
It is me. I have to get away from me.
Find another me.
Flowers!
I love flowers!
I want a flower
        to love.
Flowers are pretty.
I want one.
        A tree.
I want a tree.
A house on a hill in field by the ocean with dolphins and
trees and flowers and wind and breeze and rain and grass
and butterflies and birds and rabbits and
        There's red ink on the board
             not-board
             antithesis board
        with light from the window
             Toast.

Daydream
10/21/91

A warm-soft fuzzy reached my head
as I heard Grandfather's voice on the phone.
We stayed up and talked about everything,
even butterflies flying by in the night.
I told him about the spaceship-looking lights,
and he told me about watching the dandelions grow.
The leaves of the trees had turned orange,
reminding us that Halloween was close by
and that I had missed the Renaissance Faire.
It's hard to care about such things when he's around.
I love the black and white pictures
of him in his youth.

Waking from the daydream, I put the pictures away.
I'm lonely again.
Class will start in a minute,
and I just want to get it over with.
The grey room is pretty—
makes me cold inside.
I need to see the doctor again
for winter is upon me.

Heather Fields
10/22/91

Winds of love blow waves of heather in a sea of grass.
A seed pops up and flies away, a bird close on its trail.
A rabbit hops carelessly upon a mouse's toe;
the mouse squeaks pitifully and runs into a chipmunks
hole.
The chipmunk gives him sympathy and a cup of hot
cocoa,
which they drink complacently and stare out of the
window.
A grasshopper jumps by and leaves a message
inviting them to the mole's house
for some dancing and a bit of cabbage.
The mouse goes home while the chipmunk prepares
and eats a little dinner.
He calls his oldest friend
and they go to the party together.

Poem to Pass the Time
10/22/91

Sitting in the rocking boat,
my brain began to tilt,
and before I could stop it,
all my brains were spill.
There was a bit of fancy
just lying on the floor,
and an old idea for a story
fell upon an oar.
The parts that taught me spelling
spilled out upon the water,
and I song I used to sing
was left floating on the air.
so if you think this but a silly
poem to pass the time,
you're probably right, my pretty,
but at least I got it to rhyme.

Mimicry is the Highest Praise
10/22/91

Watching from the hallway as he does his form of art,
I record his every movement in my own.
Two worlds juxtaposed—
a doorway in-between.
One way of doing things, of capturing
the beauty on a page
is only enhanced by the other.

The Day Before My Birthday When I Was Her 500 Years Ago
1/28/92

Laughter tinkled out
the shining eyes
as she giggled
and ran down the walk—
instigating a game
that crisscrossed
on the road
and into the field,
across the stream
until, out of breath,
at the first
fair stand
she grabbed a support beam
to slow her pace
and swing about it—
then stare up
sincerely.

Playing on the Tracks
9/14/92

Shouting
   down
      the railroad tracks,
we skipped
and hollered
through the night,
black coats
      flying
as we
     jumped
the rails
and painted the concrete columns.

we went
   under
      bridges
  and over
     creeks
  while neighbor's lights
     came with neighbor's eyes;
  and we
    scattered
to the
    lights
  and sounds
of the siren.

Diving Off a Cliff's Ledge
1/14/93

Sit and dangle my legs off the edge
while turning my head behind,
I try to decide between the worlds,
but don't trust to my sight.

To my left is a field of soft green grass
and warming sun
with daisies to roll and play in.

To my right is a wooded place
with huge, strong trees
which live forever
and comfort me in their embrace.

And behind me a fog
that I can't quite see through.
But behind it I think that I can see
a stream with thousands of butterflies
beckoning me to peace.

But to my front is a cliff
off which I let my legs swing,
and below I can't quite see,
but I think it's a lake—
very deep and dark—
and I dive for the endless dream.

Built Up Walls
2/2/93

I built up walls
of thick grey brick
and hid myself behind.
I tied the tethers,
said I was sick,
and pretended I was blind.

And no one got in
as I built it up higher
and sealed the cracks with my haze.
Sat in a light, dim,
for I can't take it brighter,
and wait for the end of my daze.

Vicarious Living
2/4/93

Sitting there,
I can imagine the sound
(like the bells of the tower
on a soft afternoon)
of her voice on the phone.
My eyes close
and now I can see,
as I hear the response
to her smiles.

The Miseries of Spring
4/27/93

Spring comes on winds of sneeze
bringing with it pollen, bees, and weeds.
The salty rain of irritated eyes
falls to the ground and waters our cries.
We can't escape the itchy nose
or the pain of the briar-scratched throat.
And still we run amuck and play
from the brink of dawn to the end of day,
and sit up all our miserable nights
unable to sleep for blood-shot eyes.

When I Don't Feel Right
5/2/93

It's hard to stop the urges—
one minute there, one minute gone.
I hug myself in anger—
not sadness—
to keep me from throwing.
I work hard at not yelling, too.
The agitation keeps me pacing,
playing, banging, making noise—
just barely able to contain my composure
of normalcy
when I'd rather babble
and do the socially unacceptable.
How can I stay trapped within?
if I come out, I'll be trapped again.

Playful Spirit
6/17/93

Into the night my spirit goes
with stars and moon
and dark shadows.
Racing in the windy night
to cricket-song
and croaking frog.

Washing down a riverside,
the water rolls and rolls
carrying with it leaves and seeds
and a solitary rose.

Passing by a waterfall
where moonlight shimmers down,
it falls upon the pool
where the rose with my soul drowns.

I chase the waterbugs
down deeper
to the bluest bottom stone,
and pick it up to soar with me—
the dawning a way home.

Waiting to Play in the Rain
6/22/93

Pouring out of rainy skies,
the clouds roll over me—
and breath I take a sigh
for where I want to be.

As soon as mommy takes her eye
into another room,
I bolt for the door
and dance in the rain
until late afternoon.

And as I start to go back home,
wondering "was it worth it?",
in the sky I see a rainbow
and know, of course, it was.

Fields of Spring
6/28/93

flowers
floating
in the breeze,
with the trees
in fields
of blue and
green and yellow—
the wind
with dandelion
seeds to blow.

Changeling Child
6/30/93

The shadows dipped lower
as the moon pushed the sun away,
and in the coming darkness
they could hear the howling laughter.
So they hopped down from their porches
and climbed down from their trees
and ran singing off
to a mild summer breeze.
They played upon the swinging bridge
and hopped around the tracks.
They capered in the marshes,
and stomped through fields of grass.
Until they heard a wind-borne pipe,
saw the swamp's green glow—
then ran at their full force
to chase the music's flow.

After time
they came upon
a lonely standing hill,
and marched about it
thrice and thrice
until it opened wide.

In the morning, sun glowed in
their open bedroom windows,
and they woke with blinking eyes
and yawnings of long dead prose.

With a steely glint and an impish giggle,
the went outside to play,
and if anyone noticed the pale blue glow
that shone occasionally in their eyes,
they knew enough to keep it shut
and quietly let it slide.

Walking Through the Woods on a Dark Night
7/13/93

Before me walks the confidence of youth,
and ahead of him, the confidence of age.
And me, I walk behind
tagging along when I remember to
and bounding off when I forget.

The careful gait of the older one
draws me to its security,
for, as the child,
I have not the ability to think
before I chase the butterflies
or say what's on my mind.

The swaggering style of the youth
attracts me to its strength
for there can be no fear
among the one so fearless.

But, all in all, I would not change,
for I would not lose the wonder.
And without me,
the youth has no one to love,
the age no one to care for.
Without the youth,
we have not the nerve.
And without the age,
we have not the wisdom to know
when and where to let the other decide.

Three separate souls,
but none complete,
We make three lives,
but dream as one in spirit.

Shattering Screams
7/23/93

Screams shatter
        like mirrors
            falling
               apart
As the angel of light stands patiently by
     watching
     for a sign of some life~

The knife slips
     between
the fingers of death
        and falls
           to the depths
of his warm, soft flesh
leaving
     its tracks of blood
behind
     for some unsuspecting woman to find—

And the sky turns black with rage
as the echoes of a last caught soul
go careening through the night
waking all in its path
shouting
in frustration to be heard
outside the walls
of his solitary world.

End-Stop
9/8/93

Spiraling down,
the light up ahead waving good-bye;
and the laughter like bells
I cannot reach.

A well placed hand
to pull me out
descends
than snaps away
as the light grows smaller
and disappears.

And the bells become a funeral dirge.

And Even Worse—We've Traded Our Trees for
Concrete
11/10/93

Sleepy, hazy, life today.
Why do we bother anyway?
All the world has gone to hell;
going to school won't make me well.

You see, my sickness is in my head.
I don't know where I'm being led,
and that's too frustrating for me
to close my eyes and refuse to see.

But what I see may not be
anything else but a massive sea
of doomsday visions
with no escape provisions.

There seems to be no hope,
so why cling to the rising slope
of high inflation and less money.

There's nothing left but a downhill economy.

Leaving Us
11/3/93

Slowly flowing down the stream,
I grab a branch—
      it breaks.
I reach another;
pull me out
and dry out on the banks.

baked by sun and brains a mess
the heat just warms my heart
and sucks the wet from out my soul
while dry creeps up my spine.

trees fade out
all goes to black
I wash out in the dark
opening on a field—
      so bright—
I cannot stand the pain.

so I grab a berry
and wash it down
with water from the stream
then float along in the hazy drift
of a foggy-topped afternoon.

The Silent
2/14/94

The graceful hands of empty lands
reach out to suck the water,
and delve into the forest's green
where no one dares to follow.

In the midst, an old oak stands—
a colorful, silent daughter
of what no one has ever seen
except in deepest shadow.

And the sorrow that is man's:
He's forgotten that he taught her
when the land used to teem
with laughter in the meadow.

I Would Have... For My Goddaughter
2/28/94

I would have bought a house for you;
or tried my very best to.
I would have taught you all that's new—
better than all your teachers do.
I would have been there always—
being good so I could stay.
I would have been on my best behavior
so whenever needed, I'd be your savior.

If only fate had made it so
that I could be your mother,
you never would have had to go,
or ever, apart from your mother, suffer.

An Imagined Spring Afternoon (In Winter)
3/4/94

Hot, lazy sun beats down upon the street,
baking the concrete and asphalt alike.
Glistening people in shorts and half-shirts
walk down the road
     just as slow as they can go.
Children yell and race among them
      in and out
      through the crowds
      and 'tween the cars.
Shop doors prop open,
vendors have moved their wares to the street
where, just maybe, there's a chance of a small breeze.
Music blares from the apartment windows
above the shops
where tenants sit on window ledges,
drinking soda pops.
Or tonics for spicing up a hot Spring day
so the world passes by in a blur
of amusing images
      bringing levity to the sight.

On the horizon clouds begin to gather,
turning back in their churning.
The people turn to stare—
      happy faces turning happier—
      the thought of rain, so great!
The lightening plays between the clouds
as they rumble into town.

The water drops on tongues held out,
as a breeze begins to blow.
The shop owners quickly pack their wares
         and hurry them inside,
but the tenants over head
         just move their radios inside
and continue to sit on their sills.
The cars turn their wipers on,
but keep their windows down
so the cooler air still gets to them.
The older people on the street find a story to browse in
while the young ones revel in the pour.

It lasts a brief, few minutes
then drips its way down town.
The birds come out and sing again,
the water drips from awnings.
Leaves and petals seem brighter
         with their fresh sheen
         of water.
And the people come back out, drive on,
         or continue to play
         as if no rain had come
         or gone.

Spring's Onset
4/25/94

I remember days
of wading through tall grass
bathed in silver moon rays.
Sitting in the woods—
lost in thought—
having forgotten why we came.

Now Spring is here again
and I have come alive,
but around me are people
who never see the sky.
They sit at home,
or in a class,
only going to work.

While I can't wait
to break away,
to sit with the willow
and oak—
to play in the water,
fresh and running,
of the creek in my backyard.

There's something about
a singing bird
on a warm and breezy night

that brings my soul
up from the depths
of winter
and makes me want to cry.

Chapter 2
The Young Adulthood Years

Before the mistakes mattered so much.

A Brighter Light
7/17/94

I once was pretty wandering down;
a flower no one knew,
twisting my face to the moon.
But others spoke of a brighter light—
better than my own—
and I chose to take that route.
So now I'm known,
and still twist my face to a light,
but cannot move
as I did in the night.

Hallowe'en
9/19/94

The dawn awakens
with the cool, brisk air
of an Autumn afternoon.
Leaves
       snow
            down
asifwinterwerecomingsoon.

    Excitement reigns,
we try to pull it in.
    This night is a special one—
    to stay out with the moon.

    And if we look too closely,
the answer's almost there.
Of all the things
we think we know,
we start to see
what can't be
       here.

Hallmark Poem
9/21/94

Here's a little poem
written just for you to see.
It has no deeper meaning
than that meaning which is me.
It's purpose is so simple,
so easy to understand,
that you could not miss what I mean to say
if you had been born just yesterday.
For my simple little poem
was written just to say
I'm really very happy
you're here with me today.

A Child in a Storm
10/13/94

Raging winds tear at the trees,
blow the petal askew,
and slam the shutters of a farmhouse.
They whistle down the chimney,
and through the cracks of windows,
under doors.

Suddenly, pelting rain plinks on glass,
plops on the roof and the grass.
It turns the air grey
and makes the willow even more sodden
than it was before the storm,
as the rain splashes from the leaves to the puddles.

And up to the door comes a sagging moppet
with stringy, wet hair plastered to a face.
Clothes soaked through to the chill,
head held down in childish fear
as eyes plead out from behind the strings,
and up at the door in hopeful remorse.

Halloween Scene
10/21/94

Twenty-eight students all sitting in quiet rows
stare blankly at the screen as the movie rolls.
Nothing breaks them from their silent reverie,
not even a startling scream from the Halloween movie.
They don't seem to care, or even be slightly interested,
in the ghosts, monsters, killers, or the gruesomely
murdered.
Until, that is, they begin to hear the low moan
that isn't issuing from the screen, but the front row.
They look to see him staring blankly into space,
as sweat begins to form about his brow and drip down
off his face.
His skin begins to change, at first imperceptibly,
but then hair begins to grow and his skin bulges
creepily.
Then they know something's more horribly wrong
than they'd previously thought all along.
Suddenly, he sprouts a snout, and ears Spock would
love,
except that they're too hairy and on top of his new skull.
The poor boy begins to writhe and drops upon all fours
while his arms begin to look like legs, and his body
grows new fur.
I doubt these kids will ever look dully upon a scene
which involves monsters, or anything mean,
after staring at their classmate's new fangs
when, into a werewolf, he changed!

Time's Progression
11/25/94

A cold and gusty day outside
chills our souls to their cores
as we watch the grey clouds go by.
Shifting every day,
throughout the night,
we wait for ages
for it to be right.

We grow darker, in our time
turning white, and grey, and gone
so those behind us can come on.

As trees grow old, and crack
the yellow-brown grass snaps
with the weight of the wind
rushing the world on
to its inevitable end.

They grow darker, in their time
turning white, and grey, and gone
so those behind them can come on.

With nothing left but holes in walls
and endless, dying winter months all.
Brittle plants that can't survive
the desolation.

And they grow darker, in their time
turning white, and grey, and gone
so those behind them can come on.

And those that come next
won't understand why they were left
short on life, long on death.

And they grow darker, in their souls
turning grey, and black, and gone
leaving none behind them to come on.

Lost to Me
1/24/95

I.

I felt the sunshine on my face,
and felt the flowers grow.
I knew the touch of a soft summer breeze,
and the energy of snow.
I renewed in the life of warming water,
and rejoiced in the moon's soft glow.

II.

Then came a wind by dark breath blown
that rustled through the trees—
with it a song that stole through the wood
and shriveled all the leaves.
It reached my heart, went further still,
and stole my soul from me.

III.

The moon's gentle light I do not know,
I cannot feel the sea.
The flakes that fall are now just snow,
I've lost the summer breeze.
Flowers no longer touch my soul,
the sun is gone from me.

The Warrior
1/31/95

The warrior stands with graceful state.
The angel adds its peace.
It doesn't stop the angry pace,
the staccato gait
of one who feels the fight is his
and simply cannot wait.

And surely it was—
if it was anyone's—
but no one would let it go.

And he fights with a passion
even the angel cannot subdue.
He fights for all he has
and all they've taken away.
And, in the end, he wins—
as if it were ever in doubt.
Indeed, the fight was his,
no matter what it took.

And it took all—
the heart and soul—
of the warrior before he let it go.

Valentine's
2/14/95

Here's a flower
just for you—
the only one you'll get—
meant to tell you
I'm still glad
that we ever met.

The Day Before the Storm
3/12/95

Dusty, cloudy morning;
fades into darker grey,
a flat and almost solid color
you think you might could touch.

And the urges come upon you,
as you stumble out the door,
to a vast array of trouble
you long to be looking for.

The empty fields—they call to you;
the empty house—it sings;
the railroad tracks—they beckon;
the running creek—it only pleads.

"Come play with us," they all say,
"come smell the flowers,
the rotting wood,
the smell of metal against the rain."

Though you have a lot to do—
your homework, chores, and jobs—
the voice is much too powerful
to ignore for very long.

So then you find yourself outdoors
stumbling through the grass,
wading through the water

to see the empty house.

Then you end your day
looking at the stars
as you stumble on and off
the railroad track's old and rusty bars.

Or Did It?
3/14/95

The thing within the closet is what worries me the most.
I sleep beneath the comforting eye of an o p e n window
just in case I have to make a fairly quick escape.

I don't know if its eyes are yellow—maybe they are
green.
But I do know one thing for certain, and that is that it's
mean.
It stares at me all night so that I never sleep.

I really think it's beginning to get the very best of me.
I sleep all through my classes, and the kids think that is
funny.
I don't know what to do about this awful fantasy.

So here I sit, all huddled in my corner, while this
phantasm
wrecks in me all of what is left of what used to be
heroism,
and I wait patiently for the sun's gentle rising.

And once the sun is up, I think today I simply must
discover out that creature before the fall of dusk.
So quietly I creep to the closet and yankthedoorinarush!

What I see there defies my fear and quite enrages me;
for the only thing within my closet is an innocent stuffed
sheep.

So it seems, rather ridiculously, the sheep caused all my grief.

Becoming
3/28/95

Weighing
       down
            with pressure
until the sinking in
       envelops me
and   I   encompass   it.
Knowing not the touch and feel
as light as gentle winds
blowing through the night—
yet knowing...It is somehow me.
And the letting
         go
an EXPLOSION
that p
    o
      u
       r
        s it out
and lets it in

until
      there is no difference.

The Difference Between Day and Night
4/13/95

Paralyzed with fear,
I run throughout the house
slamming home the bolts
and turning latches on windows.
Outside, I hear the howl,
an echo of my gasping mind
(neither that nor my own sound
will cause either man to wake).
Then the first scratch upon the door,
a snarl by a window.
I think that it must break on through,
and I will not escape—

But wait!

My saving grace arrived,
but with a bitter edge,
for I am no less terrified
than when in that doomed house;
and though logic makes it clear
which (of house or apartment) is real,
still I feel one is the other
and in neither will one hear my appeal.

Growing Old
10/3/95

The ancient rise of hills of heather,
the ageless fields of green,
bring back a sense of memory
I've never really seen.
Like curling with a favorite book
to walk a path of kings,
the excitement of our every-days
does not seem to leave.
I'll never tire of the twice-read pages,
or the ones I've yet to read.
The magic of those hills and hollows
won't from my memory fade,
as with every passing year
we'll never seem to age.

On My Love
3/30/96

Overcast skies on shrouded streets
can't keep these sweet thoughts from me.
I've waited time into the end,
and I can wait it over again...

I've seen the flowers in the fields
-- the poppies in his greenhouse—
and none of that could keep him here—
his heart just pulled away.

But I can't love him any less for leaving,
and though forever, I'll not love him less
when next I get to see him.

So I can wait out all time's tales
till your next return to me;
for in my heart you will remain,
and my love you'll always be.

Battles
between 4 & 6 of '96

A parry, a dodge,
a formal retreat.
Awaiting on hills,
the quick upward beat
of calls to the charge—
no hope of defeat.

For Christian
6/29/96

This bear was "Baby" before you were born.
He's been around awhile, and may look worn,
but he's also been lonely—in need of a home
with someone his age so he won't feel alone.

So, much as I love this scruffy ol' bear,
it seemed only right that he should come here
where Christian and Baby can company keep
and neither need ever without a friend be.

Someone Else
11/12/96

Someone Else's books line their shelf.
Someone Else's hands caress their rocks.
Other People's beds sit in their rooms.
Does a lounge chair still sit on the left?
And what resides in the "Museum Room"
where Grandfather kept his relics?
I their furniture is gone—
       What happened to Grandmother's chair
       which sat empty those three years?
What is left of all I knew and loved?
Now that Someone Else lives there...

And who cares for his turtles
since in his yard play others?

Fishing
6/3/97

Cast the long line out,
and let it sink
down,
down,
till it hits the bottom
and waits
for the sleek, satin darkness to slink swimmingly by
and see it
put it in his mouth and sit.
He doesn't swallow yet—
he feels
the curves
the edges
a prick and out it goes.
All soft
one quick swallow
and he's yours!

Carey—All Grown Up?
9/1/98

Carey of the sunset time,
we traded stories
between
talks of doctors
and of hospitals
and why I seemed so lame.
I looked in on you
Once—
or twice—
and despite the difference in our age,
was proud to call you friend.

It wasn't fair,
the life you pulled.
When you needed love the most,
the most important left you lone,
to find there's nothing more.

Even I stopped checking in.

So you let go as well,
and now I find you lost.

Perhaps there's nothing now
that I can do
but watch you fall
and be proud to call you
friend.

A New Book
10/7/99

The electricity of August in the air,
the smell of Halloween on the wind,
the dark clouds that come rolling in—
it almost takes you there—
to that place Bradbury found
for two little boys and a circus come to town,
or somewhere far away:
Hyperion, Pern, or Perelandra.

Leaving down the library stair
always brings that energy here—
the static snap and cartoon color shades
that make a normal day seem so...
Somehow more alive!

Escape into the feel of Fall
by way of, around, and into
a brand new tale.

1,000,001st Ode to Spring
4/5/2000

Spring is such a lovely season
it seems the virtue-extolling number
would come to "everyone," or just under,
so here's mine-- #1,000,001.

(Apparently, I can't help glorifying
when all from brown to green is turning.)

It's only one more lousy rhyme
to add to that ode collection
--dust traps, one and all—
for none can truly equal
a single ray of sunshine.

All Are Precious
4/12/2000

Many hearts were broken
when, on butterfly wings,
your souls were taken,
and, though I never knew you,
driving by your memorial
reminds me that in what I do
I must for all be cautious,
for even those I do not know
to someone must be precious.

Sharing Me
7/19/2000

A word, a whisper, a silent request
as seen by your eyes and by my behest.
A look on the world that none save I
       ~ now you~
perceive.
To see
through the light of the afternoon sky,
to know what, underneath it all, lies—
and no one else sees what I have seen
'cause everyone carries a different dream.

Autumn Time
10/23/2000

Two boys play in a schoolyard,
after hours silence broken
by creaking hinges on slide and swing
and by laughter falling
like the leaves of Autumn trees.
Running
through those mounds of leaves,
all that matters here—
two boys and what they share.

Time goes, and so do boys—
to schools, to jobs—
to lives of their own.

And now, in their minds
the schoolyard is quiet.
No squeaking merry-go-round,
no see-saw thumping softly.
Just leaves falling to ground
with no laughter to guide them down.
Both afraid to stop and stay,
afraid it won't be the same
and only silence will remain.

Because time goes, and so do boys—
to schools, to jobs—
to lives of their own.

But late in October
with the world colored orange
and the start of a frost,
two men forget their reticence
and in the fading light
laughter can be heard
swinging in the night,
bouncing in the piles of leaves
as fifty turns to five.
Because as time goes, and boys go—
to schools, to jobs, to lives—
some also find
that time will bring us home.

Winter
1/19/2001

Cold, brisk breeze
in from the shore
as the ships begin to moor.

Aftermath
9/18/2001

All the pretty words
will never make it better
as one horrible thing
begets another.
You'd think there'd be some other way,
but, for all your thoughts,
there isn't.
And so we send those we love
to fix our broken lives
by breaking theirs and others'.
And, for all that we know it must be done,
each day it still seems harder.

The Wedding Gift
12/2001

This was the first book
I read by myself.
I've bought it for others,
but this is THE book
I held in my hands as I read
(at age five)
for my kindergarten class.
I couldn't understand then
why the tree put up with the boy.
I knew the reason was important—
it took me years to understand—
but finally I knew.
The answer was something
that I learned from you.
Fourteen years
(or more)
I've loved THIS book,
and now
I give it to you—
for you are my "boy."

And I am happy.

Chapter 3
The (First) Married Years

Wherein so many red flags were ignored.

Broken Angel
6/15/2002

I'm an angel with a broken halo,
and feathers torn from my wings.
My robes are not as white as they used to be,
my face is not as clean.
But, for all that, I'm an angel still,
and so maybe even broken angels
share in grace as well.

Winter Night
1/11/2003

The snow is flurrying lightly down now
making the night a little more bright.
Coffee makes its rounds,
a deck of cards come out,
and we settle in for the night.
The fireplace gives a soft, warm glow
and, as if to ward off the outside snow,
we wrap our blankets tight.
The hands go slowly round the table and the clock
as we play so late the sun comes up
and, for another pot, we break
then sit back down to wait.

Tragedy
11/13/2003

Stomping through the puddles
of a rain long gone by,
let down like damp curtains
that fall from the sky.
Thoughts churning whirlwinds
storming in my mind,
trying to find the reasons
--or just a calm in the eye—
waiting for tornado season
to finally pass us by.

Catch-22
Fall '04

Superscript and subscript
camouflage the world
no one knows what's happening
in the reality between
peel away the layers
from top and bottom both
'til all that's left within
is a thin and flimsy sheet
of weak and depthless thought

Devastation
Fall 2004

A whole world wrapped up in your voice,
a single sound, one small noise—
all it takes to crash my heart
and tear my small soul apart.
I worry for you and try to express it—
ask questions so I know you're set.
I never try to hurt or irritate
but it seems I do it by mistake.
Then comes anger, sarcasm, irritation—
      devastation.

Snow
Winter 2004

Swirling snow—
      falling
         down,
    the leaves
        encased
           in ice—
All bring a smell
      of cinnamon,
      of hearth fires,
      warm and nice.
And warming eyes close
      and see
        colors
      of the trees
      and blooms—
the warming wheat of summer.

Red Lake
3/25/2005

Bang!
The report was a crashing hope
coming from the hall,
taking all our hearts
in hand and crushing
those small dreams.

Creepy; Could Have Been Me
10/2005

Quiet, peaceful lot;
somnambulatory wood;
in early morning light,

with sleepy eyes,
I look around
at door ajar,
light spilling
from inside the car.

No one near,
not one sound heard,
no clear sign of life in there.

But deep inside the waking wood
there lies a piece of cloth
that once upon a time belonged
to one who now is lost.

Ode to Ireland
10/28/2005

Sun's rays on slowly golding leaves
brings an image of molting metal
pouring in leafy raindrops from the trees;

and grass beneath that's still as green
as Mother Nature's initial roll
of colors on the fields of Spring;

with lakes of placid waters that bring
swans from out of ancient lore
to swim in lazy meanderings

under skies above as blue can be,
or clouded dark with stormy roil,
yet always a depth of angel's beauty.

All this to me so Ireland seems,
a reflection of my childhood dreams.

Vacation
Winter 2005

Packing bags, zippers close
look around, more stuff to go.
Reopen bags, compress insides
takes three people to add more weight.

One person helps carry,
another gets the last minutes;
all convene at the leaving,
people milling, waiting to see

when will we leave.

The truck is loaded,
the bus is full.
The pictures are taken,
the roll has called.

So we stand to the side,
watching the bus roll,
waving at windows
we can't see inside.

Bravery
12/9/2005

Small smiles and giggling games
make our demons go away;
brighter lives and gloomy rooms,
making sunshine from the moon.

Sparkles in those shiny eyes
make us feel that we can fly.
Delight found in smaller things
causes for us easy dreams.

So when shadow darkens door,
youth plays on, we worry more;
yet work hard to never show,
though I think perhaps he knows,

and so makes his light shine brighter,
making our hearts so much lighter.

Summer
12/12/2005

Angels falling freely down
tumble to the sea,
and wash up on the shore
of quiet lea.

Singing softly hymns of love
to Mother Nature—
her moons, her suns, her trees—
every note is pure.

Butterflies and honeybees
call to the winged ones
to dance in circular
creationary rings.

Flowers bloom and blossoms fly,
swirling on the notes
of angel song created
from the tiniest of motes.

Dragonflies hum along streams
where the tiny boats drift
in a lazy summer dream
of God's greatest gift.

Mother's Love
5/10/2006

Plant a seed in a small safe space.
Watch it grow—slowly first, then apace.
As needs grow, move to a bigger spot—
but always in an indoor pot.

Only so big has it gotten.
Worry now begins to set in.
Ask a specialist to come
to what, if anything, can be done.

Without a word, or permission,
master takes the plant to sun,
puts its roots deep in the ground,
and waters it all ways 'round.

The plant perks up, leaves unfurl;
colors vibrant, petals form, open swirl
turns to drink up golden rays
enjoying its first free days.

It's not fair that it does so well
under someone else's care.
It must have had too much help—
more than a plant could do itself.

Must prepare for master's leaving;
make sure the gentle baby seedling
can survive all on its own
with no help to become grown.

So dig it up as quick as can
plant it back in seedling land.
Make sure it struggles for ever leaf
and it will grow as strong can be.

No extra sunshine, warm wet days—
just inside with a stale air haze—
and soon the plant will be as tough
as the "diamond in the rough."

First the petals all fall off;
then the leaves begin to drop.
The vibrant green turns to yellow;
then the branches start to go.

And finally, when all is gone,
the plant its strength has fairly won.
So standing proud 'side fireplace brick
is a strong and sturdy stick.

Exercise
5/12/2006

Writer's block is such a pain.
No matter how I push my brain
I cannot find a single thought,
colored phrases there are not.

My paper sits clean, empty, blank,
no black lines upon the page.
The rows are white, without mar.
I can't even lift the bar.

My creativity has flown;
my writing skills have just not grown.
It seems that I must simply quit
and learn to live without good lit.

Beauty's in the Chaos
5/18/2006

Perfection lies in imperfection,
the small things that are wrong.
Beauty is not flawlessness,
but joyful love of flaws.
So each mark upon the surface
makes a unique soul inside,
which paves the way for a unique love
that's the truest joy to find.

Conformity is dull and grey,
a mindless automaton
that shuffles through its every days
with colorless souls and minds.
No beauty in the mimicry
of the one upon the other
after that which came before
and on into eternity
until it's all a bore.

Order seems to be okay,
a way to make things work.
But chaos is more interesting,
more alive, although it hurts.

Everyone's a little broken,
our beautiful singularity;
making our beautiful days in the chaos
of breaking our every day's routine.

Techno Flea
9/15/2007

"Atoms spinning under 'scope
seem to have a void between
proton, neutron, and electron.
Nevertheless they connect
one to another
intermingling in a furious dance
of interlocking pieces.
Just as we sit shoulder to shoulder
so do the atoms that make us whole
reach across the void and link,
dancing a couple's dance.
And as our smallest particles
have already joined,
becoming one,
why cannot we, on larger scale
also join the dance?"

"Love," said she, and moved across the aisle.

Worry
9/28/2007

My little blue-eyed wonder
smiles sweetly in the Spring
and spends his Summer swimming
and his Autumns on the swings,
but winter rolls around too soon
and snow is sharply cold.
It's fun to play in for awhile
but soon will freeze us slow.
Then shiny azure eyes
too quickly lose their glow.

Halloween
11/1/2007

Pushing their way up the walk
in quiet whisper mode for once,
they dare and double-dare
and even add a double-dog-dare
when no one dares to move.
So standing staring in fascination
at awesomely wicked manse,
no one wants to set a foot upon
the weedy and cracked walkway path
that leads to the door of the huge house
that seems so like a shack.
Prodding and coaxing, they huddle up the way
anxiously approaching
that decrepit dreadful doorway.
One boy breaks the rands and leaps
at the doorbell on the porch wall
and begins a low mournful gong
that hasn't begun to fade
when the boys all run away,
scattering like dried up leaves
on a blustery Autumn day.
Meanwhile, the door begins to creak
and then, slowly, to crack
as a wan light pours out
and a shadow falls around.
A wizened, ancient woman
steps from behind a door

shortly to be joined
by a ruffled, puffed up cat
with fur so black
and eyes a glowing yellow.
In her hands a bowl she holds
as she looks upon her companion,
"Well, I guess we'll have to eat it all again."
And the cat? He just meows.

Meeting Notes
2008

Oh, my God, can these people not listen?
He said it again and again!
How strange it is
that they expect it of students
but can't themselves produce it!

Highway Hypnosis
2008

I am so sleepy I can't keep my eyes open;
I don't know how I'm going to drive home.
I'll probably run off road somewhere;
drifting off into dreamland uncontrollably
is not conducive to cognitive functionality.

A Really Wrong Limerick
2008

There was an old dog in the street
who thought every car he would meet
but the UPS truck
didn't continue his luck
when under its tires it did screech.

Caddo Lake
2008

Spanish moss
dripping down
from cypress leaves
to cypress knees
creates unworldly
beauty.

Lily pads,
differing kinds,
from soft velvet
rain repellent
to slick, shiny
flower making
beauty.

Winter Comes
11/5/2008

Winter whispers on the wind
waiting in the wings of fall
for that first snowflake drifting
in a downward spiral
to land upon uplifted face
with frosted nose and ears in red
as leaves in green and gold,
and brown, carnelian, and yellow
float down cerulean backdrop
to land and lie upon an earth
of prickly, dry covering
that crunches under foot
as we walk our wandering way
into the cool and crisp of winter.

Hero's Heaven
2009

A soldier died today;
a hero, some would say.
When retired from service to country
he continued to serve community.
Even when struck by tragedy—
losing his house, his health, his family—
no longer able to fight the blaze,
he still served in other ways.

A hero died today.
It might seem he died with nothing,
but he had much—
a family through serving,
and those he served with know
in Heaven, he's earned the richest home.

Poetry's Master
2010

Prolific in my poetry,
I am a master rhymer.
Beat and meter have I conquered;
I'm alliteration's queen.
Consonance is no mystery,
nor onomatopoeia.
Of similes and metaphors,
I know everything.
There's symbolism in every line,
personification's a breeze.
The only thing that hangs me up
is making verses free.

Midnight Snow
2010

Starry light on snow
diamond glitter on the ground
lovely soundless glow

Jack and Johnny
2010

Jack and Johnny went to play
at adult grown up things,
and when the dust did settle there,
they both had lost their dreams
crumbled in the dust
under treads of massive things.
They went with thoughts of honor,
of medals that would gleam.
Their hearts were full of pride
at the heroes they would be.
And heroes, that they were,
but even heroes die, it seems.
Such is the fate of brave young men
when intolerance pulls the strings.

Calculus Nightmares
12/14/2010

The triangular turtle
plods through a fractal world
as I stare at the visions
of multiple divisions
that float in the ether
around the math teacher.
Geometric giraffes
and algebraic equines
lumber across planes
of sines and cosines
with rectangular trees
in trigonomic designs
that make up the space
filled up in such haste
to avoid spending time
with calculus rhymes.

Shakespearean Night and Day
2010

Night is a thing of ferocious glee
trampling through midnight gardens
and sailing a starry tempestuous sea
as the world slowly darkens.

Strange creatures fly at midnight
making shadows upon the moon
just as beautiful things soar the sky
in the brightest hour of noon.

Day is like a warming bath
of golden sunshine's rays
a brief respite in the aftermath
of evening's hectic haze.

Day and night both do contend
to be the time I spend life in.

Christmas Break
12/15/2010

Desiccated dreams of damaged deliverance
fade into a haze of unimportance
as I sit in a seat with solemn silence
thinking of committing random violence
to avoid writing essays of value and substance.

The joy of learning isn't what it was once.

Oh, how I longed for Christmas Break
until I saw the tests that I had to take!

P.S. Not looking forward to Easter now, either.

Excruciating Time
1/6/2011

I want to write more poetry,
if just to fill up this book,
but my mind is as blank as it can be,
and I've done all of my work.
So here I sit in emptiness
just waiting for a rhyme.
I don't know what I'll do with this
excruciating time.

Away Day
1/6/2011

I wanna take an away day—
somewhere far from here—
so all my thoughts can rest a bit;
a trip just for my spirit.

It should be someplace blue and yellow
deep within my mind,
where imaginary rivers flow
and leave my life behind.

Valentine For My Fuzzball
2/16/2011

Fuzzy is a special kitty,
my favorite puppy-cat.
He loves me though I torture him
with Benadryl and crap.
He snuggles up real close,
but's careful with his claws.
He may not be so playful,
but that's only 'cause he's smart.
I love my little angel kitty,
though his fur is falling out,
and, unlike my other kitties,
he's getting rather skinny
instead of puffing out.
There will never be another kitty
as great as Fuzzball is
because no other fuzzy cat
will love me like he does!

On Leaves in Sam Houston Park
3/15/2011

The men are gone
hunting.
The radio sits silent by my side.
I draw the colors—
Fall in the trees
on a silent morning
on leave from the world
in Sam Houston's peace
of unrefined life.

Last Page Poem
5/5/2011

This is a last page poem
(I don't know how many I've written);
its purpose is to take up a page
so I can finally put this one away.

There's nothing that's quite so wonderful
as the start of a brand new book,
but in order for a new one to happen
the last of the old must be penned.

So here I sit once again
thinking of something to say
that will take up the space
of this silly last page
so I can shelve it

and get out another.

Origami Gift
5/5/2011

Birds and frogs and flowers
sent from far away
to colorize our hours
sitting inside all day.

Origami dances on the breeze
from the air machine's condition
like rolling waves upon the seas
of my imagination.

Origami Birds
5/5/2011

Origami birds
colors dripping from the sky
strings of pretty joy

Blank Verses
5/19/2011

Iambic pentameter—hard to write,
especially when writing unrhymed lines.
I just don't know what I'm going to do
as trochees, I find, keep slipping in, too.
Trying to write is exceptionally hard.
A rigid form requires higher levels
of skills not easily developed here.

Holocaust
5/23/2011

Eradicated
Dust, ash drifting down the street
Empty afternoon

Peaceful Kitties Disturbed
6/1/2011

This room of your content
is about to be rent asunder
by the irritating noise
of the household vacuum cleaner.
So, dear kitties, run away
and find a new safe haven
far from the scary monster
that's cleanin' where you're layin'.

Winter's Ode
6/9/2011

Bright and white should be a winter's ode,
full of the bite of frost, and icy cold
 with bitter winds spreading deadly chills
through the frigid air—or so it feels.
Bundled and bustling, nipped by crisp mornings;
crunching white fluff, watching ravens clinging
to the black negatives of dead trees' branches.
Snowmen sit by empty front porches
as snowballs fly by an icy block fortress
to the music of brittle laughter and loud spritely yells
and the clopping sounds of sleigh with its bells.
The clanking of rigging as water laps at shells
of vacant boats sitting silently in solitary slips,
no sounds from the waves of the deserted lake;
but the local pond is full of swishing skates
and the sounds of the shops' bells as gifters go in and
out.
Packages wrapped in bright and shiny colors
bringing smiles of joy to present purchasers.
Coats and gloves, pretty dresses, pants, and hats
as people come together for the annual *Nutcracker*;
and the pitiful mewing of the high-stepping cats
who thought the white stuff would be fun for a hunt.
As the sun slides down early in the night
and the sharp reflected light from the snow glows
like a ground-bound sparkle of a star's clear light;
the night is filled with a multi-colored show

on the eaves of the houses as occupants come home. Chimneys begin to fill the night with smoky shadows while fireplaces emit the warm and comforting tone of a hot chocolatey cup of dark, creamy cocoa.

Summer's Ode
6/9/2011

A summer's ode should be full of flowers,
wild words, and wasted hours;
a day's play on water slides, and sleeping trees
cooling distractions from the summer's heat—
with the sounds of birds and bugs and bees,
and sunshine pouring through summer's trees.
It's green fields of tall sweet grasses,
white colored clover and time that slowly passes.
Reading a book in a sun-filled window,
or out in the breeze of a tree-covered patio,
with a creek to the side running swiftly by
and fishing poles angled up toward the sky
with lines that hang slack in the cool, clear water,
and brightly colored red, yellow, and blue bobbers.
The buzzing hum of summer's voice
on iridescent wings of feathers and lace
carried through the night air, cool and moist,
to the lazing ear of a drowsing face
as small, silver laughter eventually fades
to the soft, slow breathing of a peaceful pace
as the day winds down to a dreamy evening
of darkening lights—soft pinks and purples,
and the darkest blue of deep midnight.
The stars peek out and the moon starts climbing
and a sometimes shadow through the night's flying

interrupting the flow of night's silky light
as it paints the landscape, fences, and shingles
with a shimmering, mystical, silvery glow
that's completely forgotten the winter's bright snow.

Autumn's Ode
7/27/2011

Autumn's ode is multi-colored
in shades of green and red and gold.
It's howling winds and raging storms
and fog and peaceful evenings.
The sound of leaves scraping pavement
and their rustling among the gentle breezes.
It's ravens sitting on the roof
calling ghosts of the first fire's embers,
brightly shining full moon-glows,
and orange-painted harvest shows.
It's carnivals of screaming kids
who run from game to ride and back again.
It's kicking stones on the road to home,
and hay rides under a blood red moon.
It's scarecrows on the porch and walks,
pumpkins carved with careful thought,
summer's clothes not quite put away,
and hot apple cider at the end of the day.
Owls sound in the coming night
giving way to a canid chorus of wolves howling
making bottle-brushes of every cat's tail.
Shadows in the night, looking wild and weird,
lead to laughter in the day at our silent fears.
At the close of school every student can taste
the scent of mischievousness on the breeze,
and it brings to their eyes a capricious gleam
as they head home to prepare for trick-or-treating

followed by mounds of candy and popcorn balls
eaten with frenzy in front of *The Wizard of Oz.*
And it ends with the odd bark as people trickle home
and soft purrs from sleeping cats that are snuggled in
close.

How to Live
7/27/2011

Arrange your days
in smiling ways,
relaxing as you go.
Create your nights
to support the light,
allowing you to grow.
And in the end
our days we'll spend
basking in a glow.

Rumors
8/10/2011

An ugly word passed on whispers,
a contemptuous look passed through neighbors,
a wealth of outside opinions
cannot hurt in any way
those at which they're aimed
~unless~
one listens a bit too carefully,
looks away in confused shame,
takes it all to heart,
treating truth and lie the same,
until all those outside opinions
become hideous inside beliefs
ripping apart the soul.

Escher
8/29/2011

Escher was a torture artist
spinning games out in our minds
with pictures full of turns and twists
creating pains behind our eyes.

I hate to look at all that art,
but am drawn there just the same.
To turn away is just too hard,
like being in a line of cars
crawling past a smashed up train.

It's beautiful nonetheless,
in all its complications
because it seems it comes the closest
to the reality of our relations.

The Scarecrow
9/1/2011

The leaves were dancing on the lawn.
The afternoon'd begun to yawn.
Squirrels bickered in the trees
while dogs were barking down the street
when neighbors talking in the yard
felt the hairs rise on their arms,
and all heads swiveled to the sound
of tires squealing from the corner 'round.
Then down the street came a flyin' truck
that skated by a ditch, then stuck
in an empty field of waist high weeds;
the windows cracked and filled with seeds.
The driver's door opened with a creak
and out a man stepped with a beak
dressed all in black from foot to head.
Wings sprouted then and fully spread,
lifting up a man at first,
but soon he turned into a bird
that soared into a red sunset
heading for parts unknown as yet.
And all the neighbors stared dumbfounded
at events unprecedented.

A Dream of Rain
9/22/2011

A dream of rain in fevered thoughts
does nothing to cure the dryness
of the parched earth around us.
It's merely an hallucination
that brings a cooling cloth to mind.
And when it finally comes—
hard, fast, and furious—
not only is it not in time,
but the ground has not been primed,
so it merely washes all away—
dreams disappearing within a day.

Furry Frogs
10/20/2011

Brown furry frogs on lilac lily pads
gaze placidly at the purple moon
as the stars come out
on the dark green night.
The orange water ripples across the pond
as the pink fish swim lazily along;
both creatures scanning for bugs to eat—
ones without fire or super sharp teeth.

The blue grass sways in the nightly wind
as the leathery white body
of tiny bird swoops in
and lands on a branch
of an ancient yellow oak tree—
its red and blue leaves
shimmering in the breeze.

SAM Sonnet
2011 Winter

Sitting in another SAM,
covering info I already have.
So much work I've still to do,
but here I waste my time with you.

So don't yell when grades aren't in;
it's not my fault that I can't win
when someone tells me where to be,
but never gives me time for me.

I can't get my class work done
when my free hours—every one—
are scheduled for another training
on a skill I'm way past mast'ring.

So this is just another sonnet
about a meeting I just don't get.

Missing Quinn
2/28/2012

Cold and frozen far away—
we think about it night and day;
the sad good-byes and warm embraces,
cheerful looks on desolate faces.
Imagining where you are now,
there's no way to think of how
you'll stand it in a land so barren,
or how we'll manage without our friend.

What's the Point?
2/28/2012

I come in every day—
across the world
they come in every day.
We teach them everything
except how to fairly play.
What will it take?
What point arithmetic,
in being scientific,
if all the teaching in the world
can't keep intolerance in check?
Why learn English, math, or science
when history just repeats itself?
What point in academics
when my friends become statistics
for the enemies' ballistics?
There is no rhyme or reason
to the things that we are teaching
if it can't keep hate from killing.

No sense teaching rocket science
until we've taught them tolerance.

The Fall of Man
2/29/2012

Ages and ages hence
well after the demise of the physical fence,
technology will control it all.
Borders'll be set by electrical walls—
no privacy between,
for every living being
will have technology their king.
And everyone will know
from birth until you go
every step you took,
victory you made,
down to the smallest little mistake.
You will never be your truest sense of "I,"
for being constantly in the public eye.

And thus our world devolves—
no separate Hell required for our fall.

The Nightmare
2/1/2013

Darkness in the night
creeping through our hearts,
slick against our sight
playing the evil part.

Racing to the mark,
spilling in the black,
spreading through the park,
seeping through the cracks,

leaving frosted tracks
glistening in red.
Never can get back;
angels here have fled.

Knowing it's all wrong,
soul inside is gone.

Wreckage
Summer 2015

I had this dream of a life;
a ship floating on a beautiful ocean of a world.
Not a big ship,
but the ship that I wanted.
Then rummaging around in the darkness
in the farthest reaches of the cargo hold,
you came up with a bottle
and opened it,
unleashing a nightmare of storms and tidal waves
that seemed to rage forever,
breaking the ship slowly into pieces.
And still I stayed,
looking for you among the wreckage.
I searched for you forever,
but I was drowning,
and you were nowhere.
And a rescue boat came.
And I took it.

Leaving you behind,
in the wreckage of what once was

Confetti Heart
Summer 2015

you tore out pieces of my heart
with every harsh word and expression of doubt,
with every time you bruised me
over all of these years--
you took more than just your pound of flesh.
you took pieces of my soul
and left behind a myriad of holes.

      so now I go about my day
      in a perfectly normal way
      hoping that empty place in me--
      that place you ripped out cruelly,
      piece by piece--

         doesn't show

then maybe someday
that void can be filled
with a soft, happy glow
that strengthens

        what's left of my Soul.

Chapter 4
The Aftermath Years

During which life gets better.

Wishing II
Fall 2015

If, by a wish, I could, for the world, erase the mistakes
that caused the most pain,
take all the hurt we heap on each other
and reduce all the sadness from which we suffer;
take all the anger that darkens our lives,
and remove all the weight that on our hearts lies;
give all in the world what is needed to cope,
and fill all of our hearts with happiness and hope,
I know I would do none of those things
because, if wishes could do feats so amazing,
I'm sure all my wishes together collected
would bring you back to the world after you've left it.

Why You Stay
2015

You drive me crazy and make me mad
with your "get me this" and "get me that."
You leave plates and plastic bottles in your wake;
I think we're going to have to clean your room out
with a rake.

But then you sit at your artist's palette
       sticks in hand
       earbuds in
       music on
       and begin.

Something beautiful about the way you move
and the sounds you make
even when you make mistakes
there's a kind of grace
when you play.
And I sit and watch in wonder

      from outside.

What I've Learned
2015

You make me late,
but I don't mind.
I've learned some things
in my short time:

> Enjoy the snow,
> the rain, the wind,
> the leaves
> when seasons change them.
>
> Enjoy days off –
> inside or out—
> enjoy just sitting on the couch.
>
> Look at the stars,
> flowers, the moon,
> a simple sunny afternoon.
>
> Show your friends things
> they have not seen;
> watch with them silently
> a storm at sea,
> waves on the beach.

Every day is full of things—
simple joys—
and the hope they bring.

So little time
we have to spend;
waste not one minute
on anger, hate,
or fighting to fit in.

Enjoy the world
and your time in it.

Guardianship
2015

Standing in fear at the window,
on guard in righteous anger,
hoping all will stay calm,
all will stay sane,
afraid of the pain,

but ready.

Christmastime
2015

I don't have much for you this Christmas
as treasures I find that you would want
I end up giving you right away.
Or things I can do when you're in need,
I simply do immediately
without regard to special days,
for doing things for those you love
means more than doing it when you "must."
And most importantly for Christmastime,
the truest gifts are never wrapped,
or sealed with ribbons, bows, or twine.
It doesn't matter, your beliefs—
Hindu, Christian, Jew, or Atheist—
this is the time we set aside
to ensure our loved ones know how we feel
when, really, we should do that all the year.
Which is why I do things for you any time;
my reasoning for it needs no rhyme
outside the fact that you're a friend of mine.
So now, this Christmas, all I have to give
is friendship for you, as long as I live.

....and that tie and tie bar, 'cause you need it,
and some more stuff on Christmas day
'cause I knew you'd like it
and I wouldn't make you wait.

The Towns Here Are Overrun
Fall 2016

The towns here are overrun with pigs,
but I live in a banana correct corral town
so we just let them run around
doing whatever they see fit.

Cross-Curriculum
Fall 2016

In 1492
Columbus sailed the ocean blue
using the science of astronomy
and tools such as the astrolabe
to discover new routes and find his way
and ended up discovering this place
      -not to mention the people already here, and
look how that turned out for them-
and lots of stuff made from some periodic elements
of highly precious financial importance-
we're talking silver and gold-
to take back in his cargo hold.
And so here we are in 2016
        <u>-1492</u>
        some 524 years later
        learning how Math and the Sciences,
        English and Social Studies,
         and new technologies
        all fit like puzzle pieces
        interlocking together.

New Era Stalker
(or My Electronics Make Me Write Sonnets)
Spring 2018

I think my phone is stalking me;
it's gotten out of hand.
We're talking about vacationing—
maybe at the sea—
and on the next day following
my news feed fills with Florida Keys.
We said we might learn to survive space
by studying the adorable tardigrade,
and the next thing that I know,
that's all my YouTube wants to show.
And now it's working with my Echo Dot
because they both keep bringing up
the dangers of unhealthy food
like the drive-thrus I've been going to.

You're gonna have to reach me by letter;
my tech all has restraining orders.

Birthday Poem
(or How I Auditioned for Hallmark)
Summer 2018

It was your birthday,
but you were away.
I was gonna give you a card,
but they were all far under par
in describing the person you are.
But then I realized it's hard
to think the best way to say
how much you are loved
each and every day!

Jakey
Fall 2018

Jakey is a good dog—
the best that can be had.
He chases away coyotes
and never gets in the bed.
Lately, it's been hard to see him,
but when the quantum mechanics are right
you can just make him out
from the corner of your eye,
lying on the patio at night.

Tragedy
Early Winter 2018

A darkness looms before me,
lit merely by a feeble candle.
The light wavers constantly
and seems always on edge of out
and leaving me entirely
without a survival route,
for as small a flame it is,
it gives me all I need,
providing me sustaining warmth
and enlightening the path I lead.
I know not what I'll do
when finally it flickers out
and leaves me wading through
a murkiness of doubt.

Man With a Stolen Crown
Early Winter 2018

How dare you tell my grandmother
there is no hope for her?
Why (in your selfishness)
did you not tell her to see a specialist?
Was it envy—
you can't so you won't
admit some can and will?
Or maybe you just thought,
"She's ninety-five;
who cares about her eyes?"
Maybe you didn't think
without activity to keep her light alive,
how, now blind, that much sooner she will die.

Do you even know who my grandma is?
She ate rotten potatoes
foraged from the road
just to survive as a kid,
and still graduated
before any of her peers did.
She built bombers for the war—
better than any man did!
She went without
so those who came after wouldn't.
She taught us all what right's about,
but still loves us when we're wrong.
She's ninety-five and still going strong.

So who are you to decide
what the end of her life should be like?
You are not kind
as she is

You are not wise
as she is
You don't even know
all she does.
You are just a man—
given a throne you haven't earned.
Every breath you take
pollutes the air she breathes
and every step you take,
the ground on which she lives.
You are less than nothing
in a world where she is everything.

Martin's Eulogy
April 26, 2019

People ask me if I will speak;
share a memory or two, maybe—
like how we got banned from Halloween
or shared the same sommelier dream.
But my words from me are ripped;
like stars around a black hole,
they've slipped.
I suppose this is what loss will do,
leaving me with nothing to say
except
"I love you."

Loss
4/30/19

How does the world just go on
now that you are gone?
It feels as if the world should spin off its axis
with the weight of your absence,
spiraling through the void
of darkness in me I can ill afford.
How is the world not mourning you
as much as
you
are mourned
by me?

My Emmy
Spring 2019

The house seems cold and hollow.
My shadow sunk below
to a place I cannot reach,
a place I cannot follow.
And the emptiness a breach
where hope lies fallow,
a private sadness for us each.

Miss You
Fall 2019

I miss you all day
from the time that I wake
until in my bed I lay

I miss you all day
whenever I play
and with each word I say

I miss you all day
at every work break
and every step I take

Your comforting ways
the comments you made
I miss every day

The way that you stayed
despite my mistakes
I miss every day

If I could've saved
all of our days
I would still say

I miss you every day

The Challenge
Fall 2019

Bubbling green,
a sous chef's dream,
the green beans
simmer on the stove.
Watching them boil,
I add some more oil
and watch it roil—
my green treasure trove.

Love Is
Fall 2019

Love is
unlaced boots,
playing the uncomplicated song,
admonishments about shoes,
and the ER all night long.
It's not in what you say
but the day to day
that I know what you feel
is love.

Uncle
Fall 2019

You were never anyone's favorite,
not even at the end;
though some did manage pity,
most didn't—not even then.

The way you lived guaranteed it.
Always thought you were best—
and made sure we all knew it—
always all about you
and who you could be mean to.

So even in your final moments
almost no one could be bothered
to sympathize with your torment,
or even care at all—
one way or the other.

So why do I now feel
some sense of loss that you are gone?
For many, it was just a relief
that you had finally moved on.

Perhaps because I'll never pass your place again
and say,
"There's where crazy Uncle Fred lives."
Or maybe it's just there'll be no one at holidays
about whom to complain.

It's as if your passing somehow left a hole
in a place 'til now unknown.
I don't exactly miss you—
 it's just too hard to explain.
I miss the quirky dimension of you
that made us more than plain.

The Passing of an Asshole
Fall 2019

How do you miss an asshole?
No one cares they're gone.
Maybe 'cause he'll never know
the truth of what he's done.
It's not you want him back.
No one he knew wants that.
It's more that he shouldn't go
before he understands
that it's him who is the asshole.

Another Poem About How Writing Poetry Is Hard
Fall 2019

Writing poetry is hard
like pushing a mower
across an uneven yard.
Similes and metaphors
swim mixingly in my mind
until I'm never sure
if I've got the right kind.
Personification is pure—
one thing I know I can do—
onomatopoeia
is a good one, too.
But blank verse leaves me cool.
What am I to do?
I can't think of a thing to say—
not even one, never mind two.
I'll never get this anyway.

Chapter 5
2020-2021

'Nuff Said

I Don't Always Like You, But I Do Always Love You
2020

I don't always like you.
Sometimes you make me mad.
Even when you drive me crazy,
it's the best I've ever had.
I'd rather be with you angry
doing what we do
than a million other places
too far away from you.
I don't know if that's love or not.
I'm not sure what that is.
But I do know what it is we've got
is the place in which my heart lives.

What the House Said to the Agoraphobic (or a Whimsical Jaunt Down Derivitism of a Clint Smith poem)
1/18/2020

We're individuals, you and I.
We stand alone,
needing no one at our side,
and yet comfortable with each other,
safe in our world,
tethered together.

They say we should be more open,
share ourselves with the world.
"The things you could bring home to me
if you'd just go out and find them."

But we know it's not safe out there.
Even with all those people,
you'd be alone.
I'd be alone.
We're better off together.

Growing old, decrepit, decayed
together, but alone in our own ways
until some day, long after we're broken
and someone comes and takes us away—
you first, in hearse,
then me, through a dynamite burst.

Teaching a Pandemic
Spring 2020

Dancing in my room alone,
music louder than it's ever been;
no one here to see;
my kids have all gone home.
For how long?
Unknown.

My walls are bare;
nothing left there
because no one's here
anymore.

Technology turned in a month too early;
no one to see lessons meant to share.
Personal things removed already.
No more sails on an empty sea—
just junkets of information
passing over our vast distance,
devoid of passion.

Who am I supposed to be?

So nothing left here
but to play my music loud
and dance to an empty crowd.

Quarantine
Spring 2020

As I sit here for the umpteenth time,
staring at this screen –
our new work from home meme—
all I can think about is rhyme.
It's like a sunny day at work
when you don't wanta be indoors.
I'm at home;
it's where my imagination roams,
but I'm supposed to be doing work.
I can feel the job walls closing in
on this space that once was free,

and then I giggle, laugh a little,
maybe.
No one's watching me!
Maybe this isn't just some dream!
I can do other things!
I scream in glee
and let loose the gates
of poetry!

Please Go Gentle Into That Good Night (or Sorry, Dylan Thomas, But I Had To) November 2020

Please go gentle into that good night.
The time has come for you to go away;
you've raged too much against the light.

Though wise men know that this is right,
your supporters try to keep the truth at bay
so they won't join you in that good night.

Good men tried to topple you from that height,
but their good intentions couldn't save the day
as you rage too much against the light.

Some men near you have taken flight,
but it's too late; it's clear that they
will join your trip into that good night.

Brave men who sought to give you sight
can now openly raise their collective voice and say
that you need to stop this rage against the light.

And you, our leader, sitting in your pitiful plight,
curse and rage against what we pray
is your final exit into that good night,
finally an end to your rage against that light.

How the Virus Isn't All Bad
Summer 2020

We're all stuck here
in this house.
No goin' out
'cept for a grocery drought,
and even then
it's 6 feet when
the X suspends
our forward trend.
It's survival of the fittest
in our foraging quest.
Gotta get there first;
nothing left for the rest.
Aren't we the silliest things
that ever you've seen,
drowning in technology
we don't even need
until it's all we got,
and then we're hot
for something not bought.
Used to be an afterthought,
but now we want trees,
to run outside, free;
head up from the screen.
Alive, finally!

Haunted
11/2020

I thought that I was over it
the same way I'm over you,
but recently I was reminded
of what you used to do
and it sickened me to feel
the way you made me to
all those years ago.

I wish that I could throw away my time with you
the same way that I threw away you.

Creep
Fall 2020

I saw her the other day
walking to the mailbox
with a dog I do not know,
and on her hand,
a ring from another man.
She looked the same—
and yet different—
a peaceful smile.
Did she see my name
on some of that mail?
(It's there sometimes;
I've checked while she's away.)
The dog's hackles rose,
and he gave a low growl.
They went back inside.
Does she feel safer
somehow sensing
how I watch over her?

Calico Crush
Fall 2020

WE'RE in charge.
WE OWN the cars.
WE HAVE the power
to do whatever.

and so a small furry ball
lies abandoned where he fell;
not even enough respect
to stop and vitals inspect
or to move him, at least,
to the side of the street.

BECAUSE

We're in CHARGE,
and own the cars
and have the POWER,
and, so, WHATEVER.

The Fall
1/6/2021

shattered windows
shattered walls
shattered dreams
throughout the halls
this is how
a maniac falls
all those people
heard the call
all those people
bought it all
they wanted right
they wanted hope
they took out
every inch of rope
followed every
kind of trope
unable to see
the true scope
finally falling
on that slippery slope

Inauguration
1/21/2021

I'm not exactly a fan,
didn't really want the man,
but as the country today
changed hands,
I felt some relief
that our Commander in Chief
would now, at least, be straight
with us,
with himself,
with the world;
someone we can count on
to just tell it like he should.
I don't have to like what he does
or even agree
about anything.
It will just be so nice
to have in the office
someone who knows
what "presidential" is.

What Courage Means
1/25/21

Some people only see
your anxiety—
not liking crowds
or people who are new
or loud.
It may seem weak
but they don't know you
as I do—
willing to stand between
friend and foe,
to take those blows,
and, even more courageous,
asking for my hand
all the time afraid
I would say "no."

They don't see what I see—
the bravery in your soul.

US75
2/2/21

The highway was shut down today
and no one would say why,
so scenarios come to curious minds.
Did a tanker truck jump the median wall?
Or another rapper take the fall?
Perhaps a high-speed chase,
or a multi-car race?
It would have to be bad
for all lanes north and south
to be blocked off; all left to re-route.
The truth, however, was much sadder.
Thinking about another hurt driver,
some innocent struck down by some road-rager,
somehow just wasn't the bother
of learning we had a jumper.

Why?

Any life gone should affect us so,
but something about some poor soul
 so lost they feel it's time to go
is so much worse than an accident
or a life taken through criminal intent.

I don't know the outcome,
don't know what was done,
but I hope that they've been given
whatever it was they were missing.

The Silent Monster
3/3/21

lying sleepy on the sofa
watching a series quietly
the back door creaks open
creating a ball of dread

sleep
oh, please, just go to bed

no
the sound of the freezer
icy packages clanging together

Let me do that
I've got it
You just go and rest

senseless words
cause tensed up nerves

I don't understand

start recording
show him later
he'll see it then
he'll know it's wrong
he'll understand
it won't take long

but

no

charging
closing the gap
a table shoved
an arm grasped
yanked to the floor
struck
things thrown
screaming
barking
growling

STOP!

Scramble away
Phone or gun?
PHONE or GUN?

Phone
Front door
at a run

Cops coming
Sirens silent

It Is Done

Disappointment
For Ms. B
4/13/2021

We've been asking for these things a long time,
our spokesperson sending emails
with reasoning clearly outlined—
and all of this coming to no avail.
So they came to me and said,
"You ask for what we need."
And I thought,
"Surely not."
How could anything I say
carry more weight
than your careful words read?
Your years of experience,
Teacher of the Year on our campus,
must carry more weight
than I (for just being white).

But I didn't see any harm in a try.
So I lost my shit
and threw a big fit
right in the middle of the hall.
I didn't expect anything to happen at all
when right after lunch I got the news—
they're making the changes.
This should be a win,
but it feels like a lose.

And I want to scream
because I really believed
that here it was different,
that here we could choose
to be more than our past,
and deep in my soul
I cling to the hope
it's just vile coincidence—
not the color of my skin.

But history is harsh
and records every sin
and it seems so unlikely
that it would choose now
just after I howled down the hallway
like a whiney-assed child
that all of the pleas before mine
had reason and rhyme.

What other explanation
for ignoring considered phrases
and only making changes
after a white woman rages?

I had thought, "Here we are—
the twenty-first century calls,"
only to find the idea's lost its shine
and behind multi-colored masks
that seem to show progress
we've only fallen behind.
And what use my words

in a world that's so broken?
Good for mere parlor tricks,
leaving real change unspoken.

I thought that our future
lay before us all golden;
that, at least in small steps,
we were moving forward—
and I could be part of that shiny new place,
a piece that helped usher in a new way.

But all I've left now
are tears for a future
I thought was today
and fears that I'm somehow to blame.
My words were not good enough,
not spoken loud enough,
not made in terms
that were strong and said clearly enough.
All of the change *here* that my words effected
is bitter now in reflection,
for when I look in a mirror
I cannot be happy we got what we needed
when I see not a bright hope that I thought was seeded
but, from the depths of a deep and dark ocean,
a drowning idea so desperately pleading,
"You must do better; it couldn't be clearer."

Ode to Popcorn
4/15/21

The popping of the corn
in the happy snacks machine
makes me anxious with desire
for my salty, buttery dream.
Greasy slick fingers
sliding over white kernels
is the only way to be.
Anticipating licking oily salt
has me dancing in my seat.
I'm not waiting for my movie
so much as my fluffy air-popped treat.

Rude Awakening
4/15/21

Crashing on the waves of a realization
that people I thought
were reasonably smart
don't even have sense enough
to accept when they're not
(or maybe it's integrity;
perhaps they're the people when the candy bowl says,
"Take One,"
and no one is watching
they take a whole ton),
hurts.

Coexistence
4/20/2021

Cooperation—
operating as one,
existing without
xenophobia
in one place,
symbolically
together
even when distanced;
never hating that which is different.
Carefully creating one world,
exception-less.

Frogs and Dragonflies
4/20/2021

Frogs and dragonflies
Natural coexistence
An easy template

Slow Intake
4/21/2021

Feel the weight of the vest,
make sure it snuggly fits.
Clear the mask and regulator,
take a breath to check it works regular.
Fins on, I sink down slow,
down past the top level flow,
watching the silent sea slip past
until I read the bottom at last,
where the colors come sharp,
blues and reds and silver sharks.
The water holds me warm
as I swim through, free-form,
in a different world
shaped by various corals.
A school of fish pass by
a reef where a nurse shark lies.
Slipping through an old plane wreck,
an eel pops up; I backpedal quick
into an overhead shelf
before laughing at myself.
Then, slowly ascending,
I stop every so often
to keep the bends away
before breaking through the surface sway,
signaling the boat in the bay
that I'm done for today.

Summer Days
4/21/2021

He wakes in the morning
and takes his coffee on the road
in the Jeep up to the mesa
where his dig unfolds,
and normally I don't go,
liking to sleep in,
and only half listenin'
when he comes home
with new pieces of the puzzle
that help him uncover
our past.

Should Have Known
5/2021

I should have known
when we let your daughter go.
Our reasons were valid
and I wanted her to know,
but you just pulled away.
As I began tracking her down,
you said it was just too painful
to even think about her.
But all I could think about
was her.
I couldn't stand the idea
of her thinking she was unwanted
by those who should want her most,
so I emailed all officials
until I found one who would work,
and then I began to write.
But you would have nothing to do with it—
didn't even want to try—
and, so, I should have known
you were more about you
than you could ever be about
me.

Failure
6/5/2021

You know what's mostly wrong with the world?
When people step outside on a late Spring night
with maybe a little lightening playing in the distant
clouds
and fireflies flashing in and out of yards,
they fail to marvel at the beauty of it all,
at the magic of a fairy-lit warm evening
with the whole world stretched before them
in all of its amazing glory,
and no one notices anymore.
That.
That is what's wrong with the world.

Poetry
6/9/2021

I've always known poetry was important,
but I never thought the world
would ever agree with me.
And then suddenly,
everywhere I go
all I see is poetry
and my heart sings.

About the Author

The author lives with her husband, beloved dog, and two mal-adjusted (but still loved) cats. She writes poetry and essays as the mood takes her, works a rewarding day job, and loves to play outside. You may contact her at annamollyauthor@gmail.com with any comments, questions, or requests—yes, she will write you a poem upon request (for a fee—she has pets to feed) about any topic (unless she finds the topic wholly distasteful, and reserves the right to decide what she feels falls into this category).

Made in the USA
Columbia, SC
09 February 2025

53130917R00133